Early Works

Andrew Fry

Dedicated to my W.E.A. Tutor Anne Bourne

Originally printed by Dennis C. Hain
101 Newport Road, Barnstaple

# PROFILE

Andrew was Born in 1961.
He has lived most of His Life in North Devon.
His interests are Theatre, Poetry of World War One, together with The American Civil War and watching Football, as a big Fan of Tottenham Hotspur.
Andrew was also a founding member of the Barnstaple Writers', which continues to meet at the Barnstaple Library.

Although He has Cerebral Palsy, this did not prevent him from marrying Jean in 1993,
Who had Graduated from Moorlands College in the Summer of 1985. Over the years Andrew has written and campaigned with Jean on many Disability Issues. Working as he has done, first as an Office Clerk and then as a Historical Researcher. Since then Andrew and Jean have been involved with a Counselling Organization and different Church activities.

As Andrew is Politically aware believing as he does in Social Justice, he became part of The Christian Socialist Movement, as well as joining The National Poetry Society, The South West Disability Development Arts Agency and North Devon Arts.

Along side this, he has found time to attend The Way with Words Literature Festival, near Totnes. As well as gaining a small bursary from the South West Arts in order to attend Totleigh Barton Devon, this took place in the late Summer of 1988, where Andrew was tutored by John Moat and John Fairfax.

In 2010 Andrew was asked if he would take part for the first time in the North Devon "Theatre Fest" which takes place during the 30 days of June. It was also during this time he exhibited some of his Poetry, www.bostonteaparty.co.uk

In 2012 Andrew and Jean took a rescue Cat on by the name of Star. She is now twelve. Since then although suffering much illness, including a seventeen day hospital visit.

During July 2015 Andrew was invited to the first R.H.S. Rosemoor's Literary Day, and from this later attended the Appledore Book Festival.

In 2018 he began volunteering at the Barnstaple Museum found at the Square, Barnstaple. During the opening year of refurbishment he has become their Poet in Residence. It is because of this Artefacts and Curiosities came about, during the Autumn of two thousand and nineteen. Since this Andrew has Published with Amazon two more volumes of Poetry, they are ''Hidden Paths'' and ''Moor Poetry'' concerning Dartmoor and Exmoor. He now writes "Petra Car Ea", a celebration of his Sixty years, upon God's Good Earth.

Andrew continues to write both Poetry and Prose

and sincerely believes that we are here to imitate our Father, the Creator. As we continue to Carol through the colours of all our lives. Travelling as Andrew does extensively through Europe and the Middle East.

His titles are Petra Car Ea, Clouds and Clouds, Marionette, Breaking Chains, Taw Poems as well as Just Passing, most recently The Golden Hare, and Hand me Down my Walking Cane, Greystone. Memories, Graffiti Poem, Down Paternoster Row and Voice, as well as of course Artefacts and Curiosities which can be found on Amazon. Andrew's Early Works are now published here once more.

# CONTENTS

## CLOUDS AND CLOUDS ©1985

p.12 White Lady Falls
p.14 My Country Air
p.16 Clouds and Clouds
p.17 The Magic of a Dartmoor Scene
p.19 Downend
p.20 Tale of Gunwalloe
p.21 Mine Eyes to Sea
p.23 The Ash
p.24 The Wealth of a Dartmoor Village
p.27 Sweet Devonshire
p.29 Deep Forest Green
p.30 Tide of Gleamings
p.31 Faith is a Tree
p.33 He
p.34 Body and Wine
p.35 The Naked Flame (Our Teacher's Gifts)
p.37 Me, Mankind, My God
p.38 Body, Spirit, and Mind
p.39 The Rebel
p.41 The Web
p.43 The Suburban Guerilla
p.45 Known unto God
p.46 The Verse of old Barum Town Fair
p.49 Passing Iron Gates
p.50 The Observer
p.51 Down at the Old Castle Inn
p.52 The White Eagle

p.53 Fire
p.54 Grave Yards Hollow
p.56 A Piper's Lament
p.57 Scenario of a Brother
p.58 Travellers
p.59 The Four Weeping Walls
p.61 'Our Edie'
p.63 Silent Sounds of Emptiness
p.65 Old Jack
p.68 Thomas
p.69 The Scribbler

Marionette ©1987

p.71 Eden's Refugee
p.72 Portrait of an Empty Room
p.74 Time
p.75 The Farrier
p.76 Marionette
p.77 The Mask
p.78 The Last Anarchist
p.79 Uniform
p.80 Yesterdays Hero
p.81 Sunday Sleepy Sunday
p.83 Subway Poem
p.84 Letters
p.85 Supporting Act
p.86 Voices
p.87 And Be Done
p.88 The Silent Island Acorn Tree
p.90 Our Man from Mars

p.92   The Condemned
p.94   The Tide
p.96   Poor Mr. Jones
p.97   End of Season
p.99   Leaves of Autumn
p.100 The Sleep
p.101 Winter Gate
p.102 The Market Place
p.104 A Bit of Peace
p.105 Memories from the Tube
p.107 Relative's Recall
p.108 The Nobodies Own
p.110 Stranger
p.111 Going
p.112 Jumble Sale
p.113 Advent Has Come
p.114 'Omeless
p.115 The Tower
p.116 The Echoing Site of Silence
p.117 The Wise Woman
p.119 Wizard
p.120 The Silent Reader
p.121 The Foreign
p.122 The Flower
p.123 The Reed
p.124 Death of a River
p.126 Spirits of the Seas
p.127 The Island
p.128 Happiness
p.130 The Onlooker
p.132 A Condemned Man Speaks

p.133 Unfulfilled
p.135 2:53 a.m.
p.136 Dead Foliage
p.137 Departing
p.138 The Hanging
p.139 The Wall
p.140 The Funeral
p.141 The Stone
p.142 Restless Soul

Breaking Chains ©1993

p.143 Wayward Lights
p.144 September
p.145 The Baptism
p.146 Somers Fall
p.147 The Flower Seller
p.148 Ode to the Ferryman
p.149 At Home
p.150 Regret
p.151 The Drift
p.152 Walking Through the Woods
p.153 Dublin's Faces
p.154 December Star
p.155 Where is She?
p.156 The Noise in the City
p.157 I Remember
p.158 Elegy to Combe
p.159 White Cat
p.160 January Field
p.161 Heralding In

p.162 Railway Journey
p.163 "SSHHH"
p.164 Early
p.165 News
p.166 Under a Sapphire Heaven
p.167 The Waiting
p.168 Streams
p.169 Everybody is
p.170 Kathleen Mary McQuire
p.171 The Long Hot Summer
p.172 Prayer
p.173 In My Father's House
p.174 Before
p.175 The Chase
p.176 It Is Where Your Eyes Are
p.177 Lost Innocences
p.178 Titch
p.179 Union Street Sundown
p.180 Change
p.181 The Late, Late Show
p.182 The Leaving
p.183 Pew Meditation
p.184 Joy
p.185 The Barge on the Beach
p.186 Late Night Shopping
p.187 Bowel Movement
p.188 The Coffee Shop
p.189 Love is
p.190 Drawing
p.191 Summer She Leads US On
p.192 Sister in Arms

p.193 Equinox
p.194 The Ferris Wheel
p.195 The Cross
p.196 Jerusalem in the Morning
p.197 Silence
p.198 Memories
p.199 Mill Side Muse
p.200 Spent Out
p.201 Breaking Chains

## WHITE LADY FALLS

Gnarled nooks and twisted roots
Buried deep in craggy cleft,
Lead O on now my rocky path,
To a gorge afar, filled only by
Those moist and musty mists,
Shadows, ever swirling covered by shaded leaf,
Of frightened haunted Prehistoric ruin.

Rush this stream, and rise to our fallen
For my heart is in m y soul,
Where the White Lady has fallen,
Search for her not, in the pools so deep,
And long for her not,
In this bewitched gorge of certain enchantment
Oh, my thoughtful one,
Now that she is lost, in them so deep,
Amid the chilling waters,
Of those unholy Prehistoric ruins,

And how I awake and tremble still,
When I saw those Eyes, 'n' her face,
Standin' jumpin' fall.
Into that foamin' grave
Of waters white,
For 'twas death of her own wantin'
When she did dive 'n' take her Life,
In deepest depths of unholy ruin,

Then scrub her clean,

And wash her new,
Raised from chirnin' whirlin' pools
Where in she did fall,
And commit such foolish folly,
Where even I did play my part,
Amid this dreamin' tragedy of an illusion called life,
Hidden in this dark and distant shaded glade,
Made from trees in the breeze,
Amid gnarled nooks and twisted roots,
Of unholy granite ruin.

Lydford Gorge 1985

## MY COUNTRY AIR

All is quiet, all is still
Pictured in my memory.

A Magpie clatters somewhere in the greenwood,
Bringing forth reams of great misery,
And sorrow,
To those of us who wait,
Breaking the silence here,
For this is my Country air,
As the shadows they're a-shortin',
And darkness tis approachin'

Oh let us now talk and speak as one,
Like bosom pals of old,
Of seasons past and present,
And yet to come,
In this my Country air,

For the clouds do quicken
Across the dimming skies,
Now that October is in the wind
                        An' air,

Hastening the on come Winter,
Whilst her burnished tints fade
Beneath the veil misty dew,
That is the fadin' reside of Summers shadow,
In this my Country air.

Wrapped is She,
My friend this Season,
In a Shroud of Golden brown,
Lighting layer of fire blankets in the Ghostly night,
Keeping cold, and using Good old Christian Spirit War
                                              At our door,

Till all Contentment reigns,
And Spring returns,
Over Salmon leap,
Nestling in the Greenwood,
Where bells of freedom Chime,
Giving painful joy to the Deer,
Where our steps are Prehistoric,
In this my Country air,,

And so my bosom pal of old
Turns expectant one full span of Man,
With increased Skies of petrified Fire 'n' flame,
In this my Country air,
Now that October She is in the Wind
An' air.

## CLOUDS AND CLOUDS

Clouds, and Clouds, I like the passing of the Clouds,
Wisps of white Cotton are they,
Scattered, and blown by winds four, that howl.

I lift my head toward the dark awesome skies above,
To the Clouds, mine eyes do stare,
With hypnotic Eye,
There I do see tones of a hundred thousand forms,
Marching, marching, across the Skies.

Perhaps they are the Souls of Devils and Demons,
Spirited away forever and a day,
In time that have been long since forgotten
By Mankind in his wisdom.

And the Autumnal mists that come,
Are they our tears of regret,
For transgressions once committed,
Against the God of Creation.

# THE MAGIC OF A DARTMOOR SCENE

You can see,
I can feel it,
In my dreams,
Across the barren wastes of beauty,
When I am far away,
My need it is to come, Oh so close,
Yet when I come near, the vast nest I touch,
And that which is Dartmoor does swallow my being,

Feel Rock of Granite carved by wind, alone,
On Tors ever stretching into those glorious Heavens,
Listen to those babbling brooks,
Smell purple heather, yellow gorse
See dark wooded glade of green,

Moody is the magic of a Dartmoor scene,
Moments of Sun, and chillen winds,
Together with Snows so deep,
Mists which fade in, blotting out,
Animals live upon a Dartmoor scene,
Stag noble head aloft,
Fox cunning cat like, the lone hunter in all pursuits,
Then come Bader Otter, Hare and Squirrel,
Black face sheep and Moorland Cattle,
Forgetting not, that which is part of a Dartmoor Scene,
Ponies,
Magpie; nature great collector share the skies with
Hawk and Falcon,

With all these creatures who share the Moor,
There is another, Mankind,
Dartmoor Man called it,
Or did it call Man?
Casting spells over them who came,
Who first love the magic of a Dartmoor scene?
For a cruel love it is, a love so deep in depth of mood,
Men have died loving it,
Those who come in Summer searching out the know not what!
Leave, having found it not!
Return they must to find the Magic of a Dartmoor Scene,

Oh, my words are few and futile,
I cannot express my feelings for Dartmoor and her Moods,
Paper is a man made medium,
To hold in the hand,
And Dartmoor is living,
And therefore cannot be held in the hand.

                    Written Lydford Church Yard, 1982

## DOWNEND

Downend is very much an end-type place,
Looked over by a funny Castle-like place,
It's a place where the wild Gulls of the Seas blue
Meet the patch-work, green, of England's famous land,
And cry and fly over and above the rocks,
The rocks of slate grey below.

The rocks, the rocks, of ages past,
The rocks, the rocks, of slate grey,
Which have been lashed, whipped, battered and bashed,
By tides of torrents, of ever restless
Foaming white crests of spray.

When I did go there again,
It had changed, for I had grew,
'Twas not how I remembered it at all,
The cliffs they were not as high as high as can be,
And I did lay my Head upon a rock,
A rock of slated grey, in the heated rays
Of bright star Sun star, and closed mine eyes,
To listen to sounds sweet to mine ears,
To gentle rippling waters,
And the many boys few, playing in blue
Along the Sea shore.

# TALE OF GUNWALLOE

In the mystic Forest, so deep, and so green,
Between upper middle Land, and lower middle Land,
There once did live a Noble Man,
Gunwalloe, Gunwalloe, a Giant was he,
So brave and so tall, Gunwalloe was he,
He did live upon the wild Boar,
That still do roam, in the mystic Forest so deep, and green.

Oh Gunwalloe, Gunwalloe,
Where did you go?
Where, but off to fight the foe.
Lord, I plead with Thee, for ye surely cannot take my Gunwalloe, so brave,
Sire, he's all that I have, is my Gunwalloe so brave,
Says thy Maiden so fair.

Now the Willow he doth weep with her,
For my Gunwalloe, my Gunwalloe so brave.
He is but dust under the Weeping Willow,
And that old Wild Boar snorts for joy,
For he shall be Bacon no more.

## MINE EYES TO SEA

Mine eyes to Sea, O Lord,
Here I sit, quiet, alone, well almost alone,
Listening semi-consciously to the winds four that howl,
And Sea which roar, with foaming white crests of spray,
The Sun is shining at me with that Ghostly grin
As if to say, I'll be back once more my friend. just wait and see,
For we are in the longest of all British Seasons, Winter cold and bleak,
Though Christmas has gone before,
So the joys of Spring cannot be far away,
These are the things that mine eyes to see, O Lord,

Tis now that locals as myself
Wander the Golden Coast, and tread these glistening sands,
Wrapped up warm, with scarves a-drooping,
Noses red, ears a funny shade of blue,
And eyes a- weeping with the cold,
We wander, stopping momentarily to stare at Lundy
As generations before have done,
An Isle full of Magic and mystery.
When Sun is hot, again my Friend,
The shall Folks come from afar,
To bathe again upon these Golden Coasts, O Lord.
Charles Kingsley's Westward ho!
                                              I see,

Hartland Point, I do spy,

With its light,
As I taste, taste the Salt upon my tongue,
Henry Williamson's famous two rivers, continually bid adieu

Adieu,

And I wave a sad farewell.
To Tarka,
For somewhere beyond mine eyes my friend,
Is another Shore,
Where Gods mighty, Mighty, Seas do Roar.

                            Saunton Sands, 1981

# THE ASH

Don't go near the Ash tree,
I beg, on bended knee, pray,
Don't go down to the old wisen Ash,
Don't shelter there,
When the sound of thunder rumbles overhead,
For it attracts the bright light, blinding sight.

Don't go near the Ash tree,
For it crackles and burns so,
Like a hanging of Witches cackles.
And if you stand there, under the old wisen Ash,
The bright light, blinding sight, will strike you down dead.

# THE WEALTH OF A DARTMOOR VILLAGE

I went for a walk alone, by myself,
Off the beaten track, where Roman feet once Trod,
Shrouded in the mists of time,

'Twas down yonder I wondered, under the old Southern
Line Bride,
All that carries now is the haunting sound in folks,
                                        Memories,

When the sound of Steam was heard in this
Community,
When not one line did they have, but Two, Great
Western,
And Southern,

Summer was far gone, I soon came to the conclusion
That the Miller had gone too,

Taken leave of his decaying Mill,
Beside The Lyd,

Over the water by way of an old wood bridge, I went on
my way,
Frightened by the sounds of my own two feet,
Crushen the fallen Autumn
Leaves,

And so I ran, breathless into light,

To a fork in the road,
Reminding me of chances taken and missed,

The Stately home of Squire Radford I passed,
"Ingo Brake" by name,

Into my head came many thoughts,
At the bottom of Gorge Hill, I paused,
To stop, to stare, into the rushing Gorge, where "The White Lady Falls"
And "Devils Cauldron" swirls 'n' foams,

Up the other side I huffed and puffed
Again heading toward the Village from whence I came,
In times of Ethelred Coins were minted here,
St. Petroc's Church too, has many, many treasures,
Epitaph to of a watch makers Tomb, The Smithy's Wheel wright Stone!
Edmund Fry, lays here, Thatcher, and Folk Sing Supreme!
It was he who first came east across the Tamer, To view The Wealth of a Dartmoor Village.

Lydford, England's largest Parish,
That covers most of the Duchy and its moods,
A Prison was Established here, for England's enemies, and her Outcasts,

Again I paused to stop 'n' to stare,
And look, at the Castle, Tasting Bitters,
For Judge Jefferys did hold his bloody assizes,

Casting People into dungeons deep, or to the
Hangman's Gallows,

As I wandered back through the Village, friends and
acquaintances I meet,
I stop and pass the time of day,
Exchanging news and gossip of the day,
When all at once, I muse again, concerning the Tors

Arms and Doe, White and Brea,
Or Widgery if that is what you prefer,
Looking down on tumbled brook, and Granite Way,
                                      With her Cross,

Golden reign,
Beyond the Village, is the road, where coaches of old
once rolled,
In search of Tin, Silver, and Ore,

All that and very much more,
Is our Wealth, The Wealth of a Dartmoor Village.

                                                   Lydford, 1981

## SWEET DEVONSHIRE

Sweet Devonshire,
A land of sweet hills,
With small Copse 'n' Woodland,
Sweet country lanes,
Thatched Cottages,
And our Birds singing Summers
                     Sweet Song,

Sweet Devonshire,
Of babbling Brooks,
Clear like Crystal,
Silver in their fortune,
Are its slow 'n' peaceful Rivers,

In Summers dog day heat,
This is my Land,
And the Soil, red,
From whence I came,

Sweet Devonshire,
Of high wind swept Tors,
Golden Sands,
And Mighty Seas,
And all them Cream Teas,

Little Ships now,
a-Bobbing,
When,
Old Men,

Mend their Nets in spite of their thoughts,

And although I Leave,
Go a-Far,
I Shall return,
To my Camomile Lawns,
Of Sweet Devonshire.

# DEEP FOREST GREEN

See the silver snakin' tricklin' stream,
See it now, runnin' through endless glades of emerald green.
See both flora and fauna,
That do lap crystal clear waters.

See the silver snakin' tricklin' stream,
A-springin' forth, from rock so green, upon the scene,
Amid the tranquil peace,
Of slender Mountain Pine.
Which does stand, in apparent whisperin' silence.

See the naked warrior,
A-runnin' through his Jungle.
He is old now, yet still no wiser,
He rushes on by, a-chasin' his desire,
That may elude him at every turn.

Yet the Pine does stand firm, through the age,
In ground of shallow alpine soil,
Growin', reachin' tall and straight,
Sunward toward the heavens above me
Where the Eagle flies, soars and glides,
On nothin' more or less, than wafts of crystal clear nothin'ness.

## TIDE OF GLEAMINGS

I sit under Apple blossom Trees,
A-lookin', a-lookin', up at the clear blue skies yonder,
And as I sit, a-lookin', a-lookin', up at the clear blue skies, wonder,
I did ponder, I pondered in awesome wonder,
At the things mine eyes do see.

Mine eyes are a tide of gleaming,
For the Garden, is a tide of gleaming,
'Tis a-comin', the Season of joy,
'Tis a-finally awakening
From its deep state, dormant state.
Winter cold, cruel, and Oh, so bleak.

O Yea, I say,
Spring be nigh upon us all,
The Days are lengthening,
And the Nights are short'nin',
And the Bees are a-certainly a-buzzing,
And all the Flowers are a-bloomin',
And you too, my little fair weather friend,
Will have to wrestle, fight, for that which is your destiny.

## FAITH IS A TREE

The Green Man's Seed spills over,
Of Adam's Lips,
Now there it stands outside my window,
                              Staked,

Against a Wooden Pole,
A Plum Tree,
Though it could be any Tree,
It hasn't any leaves,
For tis naked,
And the days are short.

When the Green Man's Seed spills over,
Of Adam's Lips,

For a Tree I believe to be like a Faith,
As if it were a Child,
That has to be up held,
With loving kindness, tenderness, through the youthful years,
As the unseen winds blow,
First that way, Then This,

The Stake,
If it were a Friend,
Would remain,
until the time when the Tree, Or Child,
Is big and strong enough.
To with stand the winds and gales of this our World,

For the Green Man's Seed spills over,
Of Adam's Lips,

The Branches speak for themselves, outstretched,
                                        Extended,

Bearing the Flowers of Spring,
And the Prospect of Fruit,
New Life, a
And the here after,
Once again, rather like Christ,
The Carpenter,
On His Tree, offering Life,
                A New,

The Second Adam,
Arms outstretched,
Growing ever strong,

Like Faith, Unseen as the Roots go deep,
So when the Storm Cometh, The Faith,
Like Our Tree,
Shall remain.

                Dad On Planting His Plum Tree, 1980

## HE

He is He, and only He is He,
I am He, He did say,
In times, times long ago.
I am all, all there can be, He did say,
In times, times long ago.

He is not less, than what you would expect of He,
He is Master, and He is the Pastor,
Though He be the Master, He is but the server
In His Father's House.

He is He, and only He can be He,
When He did walk His long and lonely road,
Carrying His cross which He bore,
Fighting the losing battle
Which He hath won, three in one,
Long before it had begun.

# BODY AND WINE

Holy, holy, holy, Lord God contrary
Deep is the Body in Spirit
And rich is the Wine,
Body and Wine.
During this your Holy Easter time,
Body and Wine.

# THE NAKED FLAME (OUR TEACHER'S GIFTS)

See the candle burning bright,
See it low, though no fear do I have,
Once I see morning time light,
For the naked flame am I.
I breathe warmth and life, said He,
So ye may see the pathways
Through these darkened days,
When the four winds for the four seasons bite and blow,
Across the cruel cold 'scape below,
A thin carpet of crusted ice and snow
Already lay to rest about my feet below,
As I stand now as I stood then,
Under heaven's starry skies,
Shining bright, in mine eyes,
For you at yonder door, to let me in,
So I may share and bare my gifts with thee.

All is quiet, all is still,
Listen hark, for sounds and singing,
shed a tear, dance away the year,
Soon a new day will be dawning,
Soon a new year will be dawning,
It will float in on a song,
What will it bring, my son?
Tears, laughter, and joy.
I know not the happenings of a year,
Like the Babe who was given gifts,
One, two, three, by Kings of old
Towering and spiring, He is here,

Though not yet come, bringing life and meaning,
For time passes slow, and is only ours to share,
For what a party without bread or wine?
'Tis incomplete, O Son of mine,
O man of mine, child of mine own hand,
Spilled from my blood,
And bought with my body,
This is my offering, this is my gift,
Offered anew to you, each and every day.

## ME, MANKIND, MY GOD

When I was born
I was kicked out, dumped and forsaken,
Left to die,
Amid the dust and dirt, the gardener worked.

I cried and I cried,
All night I dared to cry,
To whom we owe, he saved me then
He saves me still, from what I don't know,
But he saves me still,
Have pity on my poor Soul.

# BODY, SPIRIT AND MIND

Cascading rushing waters flow,
Of silver dreaming silky light white,
Down, down, from cliffs so high,
To meet baptismal waters, clear, and green.

Now when the Hand beckons me,
And the Ox trample, onward, forever onward,
Then I must go, a-raised up high,
For we are carried, whilst He doth walk, laden heavy,
Striven, striven, onward, forever onward,
To that place which is not yet seen,
Where the Eye meets Spirit, meets Body, meets Mind,
And we wander as one Hand in Hand,
As we grasp the Palm of the crucified One.

# THE REBEL

Who? Yes who is he?
The one they call the Rebel.
Is he the one who will not face the facts,
And will not accept the truth laid before his feet.
Is it he who seeks out endless degrees of
unquestionable change?
If it is he, the one they call the Rebel,
What pray ye, ought I to do?

Who? Yes, who is he?
The one they call the Rebel.
Young or old he may be.
He stands aloft for sure,
The one they call the Rebel.
Singled out for being what others have named him.
Fighting alone, for his own conscience and convictions.
On the Street corner, or in places of Office.
Does he have sight, to see more than Men who are
wise.
Are you he, the one they call the Rebel?
Nay, nay I say, ye surely cannot be.
Do I espy the Rebel, as my eyes stare inward at the
looking glass?

Some speak of a Child as being the Rebel.
Again, nay nay, I say, this cannot be.
Is it he, the one who will not face the foe?
Perhaps, indeed it is the foe.
The one they call the Rebel.

All of Mankind - is he the Rebel?
Having ate the fateful fruit against his Master's wishes,
And so made Rebels of us all.

## THE WEB

Watch and beware, keep clear,
For your God isn't near,
Though the incey wincey spider's here
And he will surely draw you in
To his well well-woven world of stinging sin.

Because some things have changed, gone now,
O little insignificant fly,
Which were here once,
Strength, want, need, and desire,
They've gone, left ye now,
I'm afraid to say,
Though not for better, have they gone,
Says me.

For 'tis basic human nature
To be strong as well as weak,
O little one,
To want, to need, and to desire.

Some things are lacking, here and now,
Here as last,
For we're caught in the web
Of our own trap,
In people and power,
In outlook and perception,
Upon this stormy day.

Again I'll tell you true,

'Twas all here once
When time was mine
And our World was for to share.

Now all there's left are clowns or politicians
And they don't care,
For the mask is wearin' thin,
To we, and us the feeble few, here upon the wall,
Who is the pest, undressed, to them all,
Standing naked, frozen cold,
Side the Sparten Warrior, there of old.

# THE SUBURBAN GUERRILLA

The Suburban Guerrilla he's here,
And near,
Both with pickets and placards
He won't go away.
He's busy brooding and breeding
All hatred and fear,
In the stark cold grey days
Which are in fact these days
He is the mood of the planet,
Is this Suburban Guerilla
Our neighbour next door?

In the twilight hour preceding the dawn
The chorus of voices that are
The Suburban Guerilla's,
For he won't go away.
He's blooded his nose
And he's ready for the fight,
Beside the camp fires of the night.

The Suburban Guerrilla he's here,
And near,
He won't go away,
Three times I say,
For he likes to hit back
Where'er he can.
At those he sees
A-caught with he,
Throwin' sticks and stones

To break their bones.

While the sentries they stand,
All huddled and grouped
Feel'n betrayed battered and bruised,
Wage'n a war, that will never really end.
In the streets and slums,
He is the mood of our planet,
Is this Suburban Guerrilla
Our neighbour next door?

## KNOWN UNTO GOD

I am here, amid ye now,
And I know not the name
Of him who lies beneath me now,
Only unto God, he is known.

He died then,
So that we may live now,
He who is known, only unto God.

The times they have a-changed now,
The wind is cold, bitter,
Colder now then then,
And the sands are a-shifting still.

Now I turn,
Turn my back, and walk away,
And in the morning,
We will remember them.

British War Cemetery,<br>France, 1.9.82

## THE VERSE OF OLD BARUM TOWN FAIR

Oyez! Oyez! I say,
Now hear ye all of this,
All those that have ears to hear,
Let them hear,
And to those who have eyes to see,
Let them now see,
For it is my task to tell ye all
Of the fair that comes but once a year,
To my home town,
Old Barum town.

Old Barum fair has come to Barum town
For many a-many a-year;
'Tis standing now, where 'tis stood,
For many a-many a-year,
On the banks of the Taw,
Which benignly winds
Down through pleasant old Devonshire
From the Tors of mystic Darty Moor,
Under Maiden Arches three,
And out to the great sprawling seas, beyond
Where the wild gulls do mourn and cry
For them that's lost
In the bottomless, bottomless deep.

I can recall my grandfather asking
"Have yuh saved up for the Fair?"
'Twas a sayin' then,
You can hear people ask,

Just before it's fair time again,
Then they come in their scores,
In their absolute scores,
From outover you know, and around and about,
When the white gloved hand of friendship is raised up over
Butchers and shoppers alike,
Then they come, I say, to meet other folks,
The same kind of folks as they,
It's a social gatherin', more or less,
And it's always been that way, more or less,
And I hope it always stays that way.

If you are an Ebenezer, I plead with thee,
Don't dare come with me to old Barum town fair,
There is many thee to part with your dirty lucre.

There are Cheap Jacks, with their endless patter and wit,
A-ready to tempt you, with a bargain or two,
Side show, and stall,
And little Money Penny falls.

Then there are rides,
Kiddies' rides,
And oh, so much more bigger rides,
Rotating wheels which take you higher and higher,
Then take you down and down to the ground below,
Leaving your poor stomach laid low,
On some other far-flung sphere.

And now I'll tell you of one thing
You see no more at old Barum Fair,
And for me at least, 'twas the fair,
The Carousel I liked watching the horses,
Spellbound to the music that came from within,
Circling around and around on their round-around world,
And now 'tis gone, the carousel, so too has the fair,
I say with a tear of regret in mine eye,
The fair will come time again, that I know,
But alas for the horses, on their magical round-about world,
Their day is past, they are out to graze now.

## PASSING IRON GATES

Come close,
Lend Me your Ears,
So I don't have to talk too loud,
It was Christmas Day at Workhouse,
And Snow was falling fast,
As I Stood at Iron Gates of Workhouse,
In Winds so cold,
Whilst the Bells did ring out,
Telling joy to the World,
Upon that same Christmas Morn,

And those that came a- Wassailing,
With Mulled Wine and Merriment,
Brought spirits from before,
carolling of the Virgin Mother,
And Child,
Its then I knew for sure,
They wouldn't begetting an Orange,
Or Two,
From My Masters Parlour,
From behind Iron Gates of Workhouse,
Every Day were near enough the same to them,
So I thought as I Wandered on My way,
To Church upon that Holy Day,

To a Victorian Christmas.<br>
Recalling Barnstaple's Work House,<br>
Later - Alexander Hospital - 'Geriatric'

## THE OBSERVER

The Sun was not up yet,
But neither was it night,
And in the lonely half light
Began to peer with startled eyes of two,
Already knowing what he knew,
That he would fall 'n lie
Before the day was through.

                                                              6th June

# DOWN THE OLD CASTLE INN

Down yonder, we would wander,
To where the atmosphere is warm and friendly,
Down at the old Castle Inn,
There we would sit and spend many a happy hour,
Just looking and listening,
To Folks and their chatter,
Whilst they did eat and drink
Amid billowing clouds of blue smoke,
Listening not were they,
To the wily Winter winds
Out yonder door.

# THE WHITE EAGLE

Your Sons and your Daughters, they are being,
Persecuted, and crucified,
Both from the left and from the right,
Over ages which have sadly passed before us now,
But what can we, who are west of Charlie do?
Though how it sickens me so,
When I see the only hope,
A-burning bright, through the darkened Night.

You are both tired and weary,
Your burdens are many and oh, so heavy,
Yet you still do labour on alone, and shall,
Led by the spirit, which is word of truth,
Which speaks out, from within your angry soul,
To he who is, the Worker,
A-toiling harder yet,
With his tools two, upon the scape.

Look up to the Skies,
There your answer lies,
In the clouded Skies, there the Eagles flies,
A-watching over ye, as he glides,
Friend or foe, he spies with eagle eye,
Though no will shall be forced upon,
His proud but noble Head.

                                                    Poland, 1982

# FIRE

Tongues of Flame, and tongues of light,
Devils delight
Coals of black, and cinders white,
Breathed from breath of Hells deep Earth,
Of wood and forests, green and orange,
Decay 'n' crackle 'n' burn,
To amber' dreaming heat, gold on light,
On this my waning winter's night.

# GRAVE YARDS HOLLOW

I arose early that morn
To arise and Ascend
And there to go,
To grave yards hollow.
Where the tombstones stood
In lines of ever present silent witness,
Against the ever chang'n winds
Of eternal fate and fortune,
As time it did surely pass
Oh, away from my grasp.
There a-down below
Afar to grave yards hollow.

For the dead and the deceased
Are buried there,
At poor little old grave yards hollow.
Where me and Michael MacMillan
Did stand in perfect awe
At the sites we saw.
Laughin' then but knowin' now
That they cannot arise, to ascend
To see the sun, and the sites we saw.

No, they'll still be there a-lyin'
When I a-come to be a-boxed,
And a-buried
At poor little old grave yards hollow.

And did the Poet speak of this?

And say,
Death has no dominion,
Was it death he spoke of?
In weariness of verse
Or life itself?

For they are there a-lyin'
All a-ready and a-waitin'
To arise and ascend,
To see the Son
Amid His glory come.

## A PIPER'S LAMENT

Battles fought, and battles won,
Triumphant cheering stopped, and now forgot.
Honours gained, and Brothers lost
Through days of much torment.
Heroes live on, but are soon forgot,
In fading memories with the sun,
For Sun is weak, in November bleak.

Now he who stands, In Highland dress,
Is the Piper, he stands to play upon the quay
His lone though ghosting haunting lament
Out across the Solent bleak,
Upon this stark, chillen, cold grey morn,
For those Souls who are dead, and now returning.
For they're rolling home alone, across the Seas,
Draped in Union colour three,
Which united and made them complete,
Some may say, and some may not.

Falkland Islands Victory, 1982

## SCENARIO OF A BROTHER

His eyes are like Sapphires,
A deep clear blue,
They'll beam and sparkle at you,
Some may say they twinkle with delight.

He is playful,
He is joyful,
He can sing, as his name suggests,
His mind is not cluttered,
With groan men's thoughts,
For he is a Child,
With Boyish thoughts,
And ideas,

He hasn't any fat on his hide,
But then neither have I,
One thing I'll guarantee,
His shirt,

Nearly always hangs out from behind.
And never so more,
Was a nice Man groan.
Than Joys boy.

                                                              Robin, 1980.

## TRAVELLERS

I know not their names, Mysterious Travellers light,
Nor from where they come, or where they go.
People's strange, with faces, with no aims,
Are mysterious Travellers light.
Wanderin' where there's a will,
Movin' through the night,
Pullin' Caravans, of Wagons, and the like,
Under starry Heavens bright.

Their image is fadin' now, fadin' fast,
'Tis distant now, as the settin' Sun, never to return,
Though Townies like us, are still weary of Folks like them.
For they steal children, don't they?
They'll utter and curse,
Speakin' in foreign tongue of Romany,
Frightnin' ye, tellin' ye,
What has been, and what will be.
Then they leave, Travellers light,
To roam, to find their home,
Wanderin' where there's a will,
Movin' through the night,
Pullin' Caravans, of Wagons, and the like.

## THE FOUR WEEPING WALLS

I am here,
Here am I
At the place I am at,
The place I love.

All things feel the same to me,
The days are lengthening,
The birds twittering in the blossoming trees,
And the Sun is hotter now, then when you last did stand,
Where I now stand.

Yet alas, I know all things cannot be the same anymore,
For the walls are a-weeping, for your loss,
We too do weep, for a good friend lost.

You are here, amid these weeping wailing walls,
In spirit, if not in body.
For this house of moorland granite
Was you, that I know.

It hurts to come here now, echoes of you I'll find,
When I walk the space between four cold walls of grey,
And watch, listen, at every turn, but you aren't there anymore.
'Tis then that I pretend, 'twas all just one bad dream,
A nightmare which would go away, come the dawn,
But alas, it doesn't, it remains, and will, I'm sad to tell.

Here I now sit, among tombstones grey,
With the others who have gone on before.
I talk, and talk to them that are left behind.
Their distant utterings are Oh, so slow,
For they're lonesome for you, when they dare to recall
Happier moments from former days.

When we see them weep so.
Do they weep for ye, who suffered and died?
Or are they weeping for themselves?
That we cannot know, nor will not know
Until such times cometh,
When all will be revealed, to one and all.

                        In memory of a Loved Aunt, 1981

## "OUR EDIE"

Miss. Easterbrook, known to all as "Our Edie"
One of old Barum Town's disappearing characters was she,
Everyone knew our little old "Edie"
Apparently alone in this our modern age,
Born in a Century when time stood still.

Black book and fine socks she would wear,
Skirts that came down to meet the ground below,
And an old Macintosh to wear, upon a blustery day.

As she ambled her way about the Town,
On and off buses, making conversation,

Everyone about old Barum Town knew "Our Edie"
At School and into Service,
It was "Our Edie's" lot to Serve
Her Maker, Master, and Earthly Friends.

For Miles she would walk,
Come rain, or shine,
Full of living,
Socialising,
Or visiting the infirm,
With her dog, or feline friend,
The "Sooty Puss"

To the Church of "St. Augustine" upon the hill,
                              She went,

To sing her Praise's of her God,
For that was "Our Edie's" lot, To Serve her Lord above,

As well as Friends, She loved her flowers,
To beatify God house, upon the hill,
Her nimble fingers were busy to the end,
The Boys will miss her sweets,
And we too shall miss her rosy red cheeks,

Now gone is she,
Gone from this Earthly Place,
To sing her song,
In everlasting joy,
With Saints,
To her God, on High,

Remembered now,
By this Scribe, and Boy below.
Edith Sarah Easterbrook

Died 1/3/1981
Aged 89

# SILENT SOUNDS OF EMPTINESS

The home of him who lived within,
Was filled with silent sounds of emptiness,
Apart from the sounds made by him who lived within,
Those silent walled off echoing sounds of emptiness.

He dressed in rags to fool those who had less than he,
For I now do state that it is my belief that he who lived within,
Those silent walled of echoing sounds of emptiness,
Was the meanest, craftiest, conniving, old creatures
I have met, or ever likely to meet.

'Twas often colder there, within
Those silent walled off echoing sounds of emptiness,
During the winter, than outside in the cold night air.
Money and death he spoke of, friends were rare,
Though one he had, to the last, a widow,
Mrs Smart by name, and most certainly by behaviour.

Anyway he's gone now, gone I say,
He's just part of the past,
Part of our fading memories,
To be forgotten as time goes by,
Though the silent walled of echoing sounds of emptiness,
Could tell his tale of woe better than I,
For they knew him better than I

Take a look, though be quick, my friend,

For I say things can change quicker than the eye can see,
Those silent sounds of emptiness will be filled,
Then mind must separate, taking over from thought,
Leaving thought alone to ponder amid
His silent sounds of emptiness.

## OLD JACK

He'd sit alone, back against, and neath the harbour wall,
Below where the gulls do cry and circle high in the sky,
Above all kinds of rhythmic swish and tidal change,
Down there below, scavenging and chasing sail boats,
And ebbing tide in glorious amber skies,
Which burn roaring red, with flaming passion and fire.

Oh, there he would be, old Jack, for sure,
Well of course, I couldn't be absolutely sure
That he was indeed christened Jack;
He might have been called Bill or Stan,
Or even Tom, Dick or Harry,
But what the matter,
I just called him Jack, because
He always seemed, to me at least,
Such a tired old man of the sea,
Mending his nets and pots, in spite of his thoughts,
Yesterday, today, always the same,
From mornin's twilight time,
Till evenin's openin' time,
Ole Jack, there he would be,
Down by the Quay.

A-mutterin' and a-whilin',
A-singin' in songs and shanties,
About the good days,
The old days, during the bygone times,
When the seas were clean,
And the Joeys were still there,

Before the big ships sailed in,
From a far-flung shore, and cast their nets,
And spread them far to the four winds.

Take note of him young man,
Though he may just appear to be,
Such a dodderin' old man of the sea,
Mending his nets and pots, in spite of his thoughts,
For he was right and they were wrong,
Though he be bald
And his whiskers be grey,
And his eyes they are dimming now,
But he's still seen and heard, more than me and ye.

His skin was wizen and wrinkled with age,
Tanned by salt, sun and foaming white wind swept seas,
As he stands and stares in gaze of settin' sun,
The lights they all come on,
And he lights his faithful pipe,
 In the still blustering breeze that comes in from the seas,
And he turns his back upon the whispering water
To walk the narrow cobbled streets,
To the chapel of Saint Nicholas, upon the hill
And then to his bunk beyond.

His gait was wide, for he limped,
So he rolled and ambled his way along,
Pitching and rolling, as if he were an old schooner,
Bowing up and' down upon a storm tossed tempest,
Out at sea, yonder the fading lights

And the harbour wall,
And what remains of a once thriving fishing fleet.

# THOMAS

Get up,
And get out of the way,
For you should know, that time waits for no Man,
You dirty old Man.

They whipped and stripped our sacred lands,
Tearing down row upon row of friendly brick-built neighbourhoods,
To put up what?
Concrete Jungles of Mugger's delight.
Where the word friend is simply that, a word, my friend,
Thomas stepped out, and turned his collar to the cold and damp.
Thomas doubts whether he'll ever work again,
His fellow kind have seen to that.

Those who sit in high office
They say, I'll be all right,
Though Thomas doubts their words of wisdom.
For I have no doubt it will be, all right,
When our doubting Thomas has walked his road and out of sight,
And we all bow down on bended knee to the Gods we made.

# THE SCRIBBLER

He casts his magic spell and draws you in,
Does he who sits in Moon blessed room.
There at the window,
Against the dimming evening shadow
Of Western skies afar,
And scribes and writes,
On walls, desks, envelopes, and pages,
With ink and quill, for 'tis his will.
In vivid mood, shade, and living colour,
Painting portraits of his day,
Upon the virgin parchment there that lay.

The Scribbler,
And why did they do all of this?
he thinks brazen thoughts for his world to feel and read,
Because somebody said so, my friend.
In anger and pain, his angry Soul shouts aloud,
To cripple, then defend, a State, for Scribbler all.
He lives alone,
in contentment as he will, his mind and spirit captured
For himself, by himself, which none can destroy
Being strange, aloof from those around,
Perhaps a wee bit eccentric too.
They 'ooh' and 'ah' and crave for his passion and glory,
They like his word, but how they cramp his style as well,
Though none would want to wield his mighty gifted pen,
For none can see, as he can see,

Left or right, what the aim, both the same,
Utopia, not the same, as they who've gone before can see.
So he strides and scribes his way for today, into morrow's day.
Till we like he can see his mortal visionary,
Left as a missionary in the darkened jungles deep.

## EDEN'S REFUGEE

It's not often that I come up here now,
Just to watch the fleecy white buds of cotton
Cross the evenin' skies,
Now the Sun is settin'.
But rather to watch Urban Man
Guard His yard an' cut His grass,
Beneath the Tree of knowledge gained.

Though a little wiser, taking in fruit from the vine,
He knows nothing of Fetes 'n' Fairs 'n' Country airs.
For what knowledge gained,
Comes from His living room chair?
Whilst at His side sits His canine companion
There to protect His patch from His neighbour,
Lookin' on like sone great Chad characters
With prehistoric envy

So Eden's Refugee continues to feud
Over wealth immense pulsating beneath the Sands.
And what do they do,
When talkin' is done?
But praise their Lord
An' use their Guns.

# PORTRAIT OF AN EMPTY ROOM

The Room Was Empty,
Filled Only By Myself,
Kind Of Hollow,
Ere,
Whilst The Rain Came,
And Beat Upon My Window Pane,

The Noises Of The Voices,
Had Gone, Had Gone,
And I Was There All On My Own,
                      My Own,

Just as I Listened To Weather Wind Sound,
Again Come Knocking, Knocking,
At My Head,
In My Mind,
Heart and Mind,
The Dust Did Settle,
As I Ate My Crisp,
My Salted Crisp,
Upon My Tongue Of Taste complete,

Relentless Was The Clock,
The Old Mantle Tick Tock Clock,
That Beat out The Hour,
That Told The Time,
And Gave No Rhyme,

To the Fire I had lit hours before,

At Bloater Town,
At Bloater Town,
That Burnt The Wood,
To a Cinder White,
And Smelt,
And Smouldered Warming On!

# TIME

Time,
> Is a warped concept,
> It is part of Man
> And His imagination.

Time,
> Is the essence for all Man
> He just doesn't have enough.

Time,
> Is a four letter word,
> That some may have reason to fear.
> We are all in

Time,
> For we are all in the World
> And outside this World Man
> He cannot comprehend the word

Time.

Time,
> To Him is dark an' light, night 'n' day,
> Around which He has the basis to record
> The trials 'n' tribulations of the everyday
> Folk.

Time,
> The Sands are running.

## THE FARRIER

Pray,
Note the Farrier O' fair one.
Note too His action at the Forge
While the door is still ajar.
See the flickin' flame burn amber bright.
See Him sweat, as He smelts
Tempering, with Anvil 'n' Hammer
Working the metal
To shape 'n' to make
That which the World wants from Him.

# MARIONETTE

The Marionette is dancing yet
Though He has no brain,
For His head is stuffed with hay.
So He's often rude an' crude,
Busy getting nowhere fast,
Feelin' used an' abused,
Having been swayed to the right,
And pulled to the left
On strings of wires 'n' ropes of delight
Climb inside then see this sight,
Whilst the tangled are twisted and pulled.
For it is only then that He's moved to pour
His wooden tears all over the floor.

# THE MASK

Quick, over there the funny little fellow
With the large red nose,
Here He comes an' there He goes
Running around the ring,
With His slap stick humour.
He's played to a thousand audiences
An' met a thousand custard pies
Right between the eyes.

Who or what hides from view?
Why need a Mask?
So colourful an' grotesque,
When everyone's friend,
An' nobody's fool.

# THE LAST ANARCHIST

The last Anarchist shall hold Public Office,
His Mask Shall Fall,
And We the People will be like He,
Indifferent.

# UNIFORM

You who wear uniform
You have no choice,
For you have already made your choice.
To put on your uniform,
And make known your colour shown.
You who wear uniform
You have no view,
When you put on your uniform.
For your view has then become
Our State's view,
And made opinion known its colour shown.
You who wear uniform
You dance on strings,
You poor little things.
Then beg to play,
Killing, cloth rather than creed
And makin' known whose colour shown.

## YESTERDAY'S HERO

He stands hands in pockets,
Waitin' for the Pub to open.
He's just another face in a million faces,
Just one more old Man complaining an' biding
His now slowing time.

That old Man I saw merged into the wall,
They who passed Him couldn't see Him.
For their vision is blurred through travellin'
At speed,
Anyway He's only a yesterdays hero.

With drawn into Himself
Behind his growth so white,
He looks for some kind of recognition
From the World He knew,
An' the World He sees.
Though ever expectant, He knows full well
That He's only yesterdays hero.

He's had His dreams, those dreams
That did deceive.
And now he sees them in others passing,
Passing by.
He has fought His wars on many a-front
And often wondered whether it was worth it,
Now that He's a burden.
For those who are busy becoming their
Own yesterdays hero.

## SUNDAY SLEEPY SUNDAY

The sleep began to leave my Ears
As I lay still slumberin' on,
Waitin' for my Eyes to focus, on
The square World of my darkened room.
It must have been the Bells that disturbed me
I decided, echoing down the valley.
Or had it been the dawn chorus that had woke
Me?

I didn't know as I arose,
Either way God in His Morning
Had decided to wake me, with Human Hand
And Nature's voice there to tell me,
It was Sunday.

Sunday sleepy Sunday,
The first day 'n' the only rest day
For the silent majority.
Now to be seen strollin', aimless
Whilst they may.

Sunday sleepy Sunday,
His day, I say with a stretch 'n' yawn.
For I shan't be in Church, I'm not
In a fit state.
Why are my Saturday Evenin's
Always followed by your Sunday Mornin's?
Lord!
Can't you re-arrange it?

That is if you want me.

Anyway thanks, it's a nice day
There's still Papers to buy,
An' friends to see.
And down the street there's a group
of Kids gathered,
Playing make believe yesterday's heroes.

# SUBWAY POEM

My colour is grey, like the Skies
Almost cruel.
Winter shall have its bite
Now the north wind does blow,
An' the outlook is bleak.
To our obscene green generation,
An' the Eyes of March have turned
Swift with the tide,
Flowing brown long side
To this my obscene green generation.
Dig'en their Subway Poems an' works
To try an' stifle the tide.

Down Down, we dig 'n' go
Till caught,
Amid the heaving breathing Jungle din,
Come rain or shine noon or night
Into a well shaded coven spoken World of
Whispers.
Filled only by those proud Palaces of
Power, an' their spoken works of Subway verse.
Left behind an' read,
As a sneering mark of contempt
As history books they have shown.

# LETTERS

Letters written 'n' letters received
Over distance covered 'n' distance spent,
An' Heart felt sentiment
Words are uttered,
An' words are spoken
On silent pages.

# SUPPORTING ACT

The Theatre went dark,
For they had dimmed the lights
And my evening of paid pleasure
Had finally begun,
When the curtain back it swung.
And out stepped a Naive,
Into the daunting dancing gaze
Of the spotlight glare,
Trapping the dust above His hair.
They clapped
'N' I did not,
But instead sunk into my chair.
He started to play
Again they clapped
'N' I did not,
For Him who was performin'
Under His hat,
I thought His act was flat.
Though 'He' who had only just come on,
Had come on to set up an' wind up
This face in a cast of thousands.

## VOICES

Voices, distant an' thinly veiled
Chattered 'n' gathered hurriedly
With expectant excitement,
And drew near.
The party was about to begin.

## AND BE DONE

All I can do is observe with both Ears 'n' Eyes
A People oppressed 'n' regimented in a belief
Of a word called freedom.
Living in a clouded haze of disbelief,
For the Wheels are turning not, at Pit Head
An' the Factories are silent an' crumblin' Lord.

Whilst standing by the Ballot box
Then is their chance to speak,
In one frustrated act
With a tiresome cross,
Born of Wood my Lord.
Though how many listen
Amid this well communicated crowd?
No need to answer me,
Although curious by all means.

For I am done,
Just as those who went once
To fight the Hun's boomin' Gun
There at Verdun.
Now Bricks, Walls 'n' graffiti
Get edited,
Because we too are as the Mole
Who takes and feeds from the soil.

## THE SILENT ISLAND ACORN TREE

Wet was the day
Rainy day, and Monday.
When I did kick an' scuff at the leaves
That had fallen from the trees,
Neath the cool breezes blow.
When days roll into Weeks an' Weeks
Into Months and begotten Years.

For I am sick, sick to death,
Tired an' weary,
Weary an' worn
Tattered an' torn,
To shreds of life
Here after death,
All duty bound.
Where floating flutterin' fools
Exist only for the silly most rules.

What is the purpose?
What is the time?
In this realness of rhyme.
When moody is the home
Of the silent Island acorn tree,
That has cast its shadow a far to Sea.

Both opening an' closing
Rising an' falling,
To the tide about
This shrouded shaded silent Island of an acorn tree.

That has stood through time
Above all benign an' mindless rhyme,
In all its perfect honesty.

Where Cathedrals an' temples
They stand an' they lie,
In ashes of ruin.
Our silent Island acorn tree
Will still be standing eternally.

## OUR MAN FROM MARS

You Ship of the Sea
Tossed by tempest green,
Undecided blown by the winds
And as mad as the mad March Hare.
Swayed by Scribes 'n' learned Scholars
Is our Man from Mars.

He stands astute a-fixed to His chain
Trapped like a thief,
Behind your bars of the mind
Within your choking Self.

There you see your scaffold
Which others have built.
When the page is opened
Your life is read.
An' the words that you write
Black on white,
Has surely condemned
This our Man from Mars.
If the rope should swing 'n' break to cut
In all your honours gained
First rather than last.

But what of this you God of War?
Crossing the Moat.
Now that you've left your Circus
Ring,
Amid the Heavenly stars.

You Clown among fools at least you can laugh,
Leavin' the bridge all down
The gate is clear 'n' wide,
To tempt an' sway the Demon
To be my guide.

                                                   The Character,
                                   And The Meaning of His Name.

# THE CONDEMNED

Damp, dark is the room
The cold, cold room.
And blank are the walls
For walls that surround,
His cold, cold room.

In a World which is square
With window bar'd an' freedom taken
He's still there, dragging His chain
Attached to His mane.

Go visit Him by day
Or dream time sleep.
Then transfuse your blood
An' give Him life,
Dear Daughter.

So that He too might write,
For He read your letter again last night
Before the Sun did sink from His sight.
Then sees each psychedelic page unfold,
For it is better not to know your direction
Than for a Demon to be your guide.

Says this hand, a conscience pricked
A Prisoner oppressed and now Condemned
For once Condemning,
By word 'n' mouth.
But the truth it speaks louder

From this action alone.

# THE TIDE

I used to live here once
Before the salted Seas
Washed my print from these sands.
I don't remember much about it though
Of course for I was younger Then.
And what I do recall
Is just the occasional event
Brought back to life,
Through the odd photograph
Or what has been said.
At least, some may say,
It hasn't changed all that much
On the Face of it, anyway.
Though alas it has, would be my
Reply,
With the changin' of the tide.

Men they've left their rusting rails
Taken leave, now the steam has gone,
Taking with it the real old characters
Of both Land an' Sea,
Which are fewer now with each turnin' of the tide.
For now the Village it's run
By the OK yah set,
An' they don't care or really want to know
With their yellow Wellies,
Red Setters.
And their talk is of Yacht Clubs, Sailing Dinghys
Parties, and the inevitable F. T. Index.

Neither party understands the other
Nor will they,
For they lead separate lives
Divided like the Villages,
By Water 'n' Moon tide 'n' torrent
Ebbing 'n' flowing.
My mood is mournful,
Grey like the wall
An' cold as Winters cruel airs.
The Bridges Men build are clever
Though look a bloody sight,
Stuck across the estuary there.
So much for tourism
What's it ever done?
But condemned an' ruined the character
Of the place.

# POOR MR. JONES

Mr Jones, He just sits an' nibbles
At His limp Pork pie,
Taking angry sized bites
From a home grown Tomato,
Of them He's proud
Is poor Mr Jones.

Whilst He just wistfully dreams
Of last years holiday,
Whilst planning next years Summer holiday
Poor Mr Jones.

He would dearly like to be able to take
The Wife 'n' the Kids to Nice or Greece.
Though He knows He will have to settle
For a wet Weekend in Wessex.
For the Taxman always wants more,
An' then there's the mortgage
Dear Mr Jones.

Time is never your own
For you're bound by a bond,
Mr Jones.

## END OF SEASON

T'was end of season now
Anybody could see that.
The only thing that remained the same
Was the Town Hall clock,
Turning upon the hour
Recording Men an' their lives,
In seconds 'n' minutes.

Those who walked along the Prom
And sat in the Park,
Eating Ices from the Parlours
Protected themselves from the
Blusterin' breeze.
Were O.A.P.s an' Honeymooners
On cheap day returns, Special excursions
An' Weekend breaks.

For now vacancy signs
Could be seen,
And were now common place.
In a Town that had always
Been in decline,
And lived its life but a few Weeks
A year.
Amid flakin' paint,
An' pavement crack
Of colours drab,
Sea blown winds
An' dulling Skies.

As cafes close
With silly little Nick-nack shops
All sellin' kiss me quick hats.

Now to die an' not to be mourned
For Summer She will surely live again.
When Winter has finally done its grievin'
For those who passed along
The season 'end' way.
And would surely be passin' again,
When time has turned the hours recording.

# LEAVES OF AUTUMN

Leaves of Autumn, damp
Wistful winds make 'um' rustle,
Sudden turf,
Colours dark, rich 'n' reds,
Golden browns, sheds,
Speaks of dreams fulfilled,
Of hedge row harvests,
Growing tired beneath veiled skies
Empty of song,
Turns expectant,
Dies to cruel winter.

## THE SLEEP

'Tis a cold raw Mornin'
Month not known,
Nor is it necessary to know.
For the Town 'tis asleep
In moderate hibernation
Under a thinly veiled blanket,
Now that the Tourists have gone
Taken leave of their Summer retreats
Down along the Water Front.

And those that stay on
Don't venture far,
From both fire 'n' hearth
So are condemned to wait, reluctant
For tides of torrents ever returnin'
Both ebbin''n' flowin'.
Like the good Rebecca
Lays upon Her side,
And waits for the tide.

## WINTER GALE

The wild winds whistle 'n' blew,
In from the north 'n' west,
Whining g and whipping,
The light,
The beacon light,
Around the Peninsular blew.

Cracking like a Heavenly,
Timpani Drum,
Timpani Drum.

Over the Heads of those who slumber 'n' rest,
                             Slumber 'n' rest.

A - waitin' lightenin's,
Challenge,
Come Mornin's light.

# THE MARKET PLACE

Empty is the Pantry,
Not a crumb
Not a fated morsel
Is there left for us,
Our cupboard is bare.

No longer does it produce
All our loves labour'd fruits.
For the season no longer turns,
Our country 'tis sunk after bathing
In the wake of its own glory.

The young and the skilled
They've paid their fares
An' now they've taken their wares,
Leaving one to stand an' stare
With many a-unforgotten care.

Kicking at the floor is He,
The lone survivor,
Or maybe stayer,
Wasting His time
Doing time
Listening to the noise that was
In the silence of the Market place.

Where there's no hope,
Where there's no choice,
Starving His Belly,

Starving His Soul,
In a fruitless choiceless
Market Place.

## A BIT OF PEACE

With the sound of the screaming War Bird
Splitting the air above my Head.
Where is the silence that a different generation
Would have known?
Now that the World turns toward the Eagle 'n' the Bear
For a bit of peace that passes all understanding.

In days of yore Man killed Beasts 'n' Men
An' did not think what method to use,
For He had to eat 'n' War was War.
Now times are different
War is still War,
And He still needs to eat.
Though how far shall we go
To satisfy our crazy hunger?

## MEMORIES FROM THE TUBE

Sat the Woman in front of Her screen
Watchin' movin' pictures,
Of marchin' Men goose step
Down memory lane.
On celluloid film
Colour not shown
Shot, caught an' trapped, frame by frame
For time to keep,
Like the faces She's seen
On cattle truck train.

Speeded 'n' blurred
These are Her memories,
The memories She's seen.
In living black an' white
Of war 'n' strife
An' Hell on Earth.
As was times then,
And memories now, more on want.

Resurrected from the can
An' brought to life in living death
Memories from the tube,
With floods of tears
Come blood river run.
Pale 'n' gaunt they hung
Meddling with the chosen one.

Yes you did run

And now your tongue
Your native tongue
Is divided 'n' cast.
It's then we ask under wire 'n' wall,
Why did it happen?
And why do you weep so, handkerchief in hand?

Is it for the untold dead of a Nuclear age?
Only to have Missiles strewn in the street,
Is this the reason why they died?
Reviewing memories from the tube.

> World War Two,
> And The Misplaced
> Peoples of the World.

## RELATIVE RECALL

"Crow"
Today we went to a place that is no more,
Where Boys once ate tea an' cake.
Whilst Uncle Sam played an' prepared for War
Down beside the shore,
Under the phosphorescence
Of the crescent shape Bow.
Except for the pictures by the open door
Memories aren't to be found 'n' recalled
By the turnin' of Fossilised stones,
An' tidal wash erosion.
But in the talk of a relatives recall
Now grown, the door is closing,
An' the Keeper of His light has taken leave
"Crow, Crow, a-bleak Crow".

          A Memory of Crow Point Light House.

# THE NOBODIES OWN

Have you seen them?
The poor in Spirit,
The lonely
And the down and out.
The Nobodies own, condemned
Neath their rain soaked cardboard
Covers.
Come rain or shine,
Winter or Summer
They're there,
The Nobodies own
Waitin' for Charity to call.
They've run, they've hid
And now there's nowhere left to hide
From the Nobodies own,
Especially when concerning yourself.
Running and hiding, driving down cul-de-sac's
Living on loves memories,
Whilst the seasons turn and colours shades
Fade, on how things were once.
These are the everyday lives
Of those who left their life.
Though still go on exciting unnoticed
In the darkened midnight hour,
Of our day.
Cos they're the Nobodies own
With strings all broken,
Tattered 'n' torn.
Drinkin''n' drownin'.

Condemned is their sight,
A vision they see.
A bottle so full,
As full as could be.

                Testimony to Men and Their Caring.

# STRANGER

The Face had changed
From that I knew.
It had been unmasked
Defaced 'n' deranged,
For whence in silence it spoke.
Maybe it was because
It too was empty,
Like the wine glass
There amid the table bare.

# GOING

Between four 'n' six the exodus takes place,
People start to leave in Buses, Cars, Trains an' Trams,
They hurry having fulfilled their duty,
Homeward, away from the dark,
To their three Bedroom semi's
To live their uncaring esoteric lives,
To eat their Microwave meals
Then to watch the bubble box,
Till bubbles come out of their Ears.

## JUMBLE SALE

Other Folk's rubbish,
Collected and gathered
For Sale or Work,
In countless scores of draughty Parish
Halls.
For ever held it seems to me on some
Wet an' windy Winter's afternoon.
When local Kids have grown bored
And stopped playing with last years
Christmas toys.
An' now they're to be sold
Half battered 'n' broken,
To some more deservin' Charitable cause
That the local Parish Priest has in mind.

## ADVENT HAS COME

Shadows lengthen as darkness falls
Under dreary Skies.
Shoppers wander bedraggled 'n' wet,
They hurry an' scurry
Toin' an' froin', Lookin' an' listenin',
In windows decked
With gifts of festive fun,
Now that Advent has come.
Though what of the Man
Who has no fun?
Who lays in the gutter
An' lays in the dust,
An' begs to be fust
For His much needed crust,
Among Town an' Country waste.
Far from the jokers'
Well predicted unproductive
Plains of well conditioned vanity.
Bland band play your tune
Under dreary Skies still yet.
The People walk waltzin' 'n' wanderin'
What to buy their Child still yet,
Further gifts this Advent tide.
When gift He brought, that perfect Clown
Oh Catholic Church few did recognise,
The significance of Blood 'n' Wine.
When in the Circus ring
They hung Him high,
Leaving Bread to rot, to die.

## 'OMELESS

Early one mornin' 'twas I
That wandered both far an' wide.
Drinkin' sleepin'
an' eatin'
To beg for a bed,
To beg for a 'Ome
Far away from the foot-lights gay.

# THE TOWER

The Drum does beat,
And I see the far Tower
Bathed in a shaft of pure Sun.
Where distant Skies meet Earth
An' the grass 'tis ever green,
In this my Mornin' time light.
Though what would be my view
If condemned this Maverick am I,
Amid the Tower, O' yours encircling?

# THE ECHOING SITES OF SILENCE

Old ruined Towers 'n' Castles I see,
Where mournful mists draw down upon this
Frightened land,
Now protect the echoing sites of silence.
A Carrion Crow does cry where once battles
Were waged 'n' won 'n' Men did die,
Against Saracen arrow 'n' Round Head foe.

## THE WISE WOMAN

Have you seen the wise Woman,
The wise Woman of Willow Woods?
With fingers an' nails like talons an' claws,
Who goes on weeping still
Beneath Her weeping Willow,
Side the rivers of sorrow.

She's old now, is the wise Woman,
The wise Woman of Willow Woods
With a mixture of assorted warts
Upon Her nose.
And hair so thin and white
That hangs all tangled an' lank.

Some believe She's a witch
An' say, She has cursed 'n' killed
Preying on the young.
Whilst I can tell a different tale
From a much more earlier verse.

That She was a Maiden, a Maiden so fair,
Is the wise Woman of Willow Woods.
Who once did love a Noble Man
Who went to fight the Foe,
And was killed by a blow
When once youth did walk at Her side.

Before Her Lord turned deaf
And answered Her not,

When the Devil came a-calling
With age to weary, beneath the Willow.

# WIZARD

Ash falling, the remains droopin'
An' smoulderin' on.
Perched in the corner, one step removed
Scrawlin' an' scribbling, still life.
His pictured painted, recording
His colourful characters created,
Whilst drinking liberally.
His Bow is drawn
With Arrow to pierce
The skin,
A love for life
Amid His image torn mind
In this His Worldly Kingdom of dreams
An' rhymes,
He is the spirit of Camelot.

## THE SILENT READER

I sit 'n' I write my Poems 'n' Prose,
But for whom do I write?
These my Poems 'n' Prose.
Let it be not for nobodies Eyes
That I write these my Poems 'n' Prose.

For I have seen 'n' heard
Of silent Reader's,
Here upon this midnight hour
Readin' my word
For once I'd writ.

For 'twas never meant to be spoken aloud,
But entwined in the Soul
And heard in the mind,
These are my Poems 'n' Prose.
Words that I did hear
An' you did fill
Almost to my will.

Now my silent reader
Speak to me, as if you've spoken
Aloud from the stage to the floor
Where our paths may tread 'n' reach
A-far
From this silent midnight hour.
Where the Poppies grow
And I might write at will.

## THE FOREIGN

Blossom was yet to appear,
Whilst the Golden Daffodil was trumpeting in
The sounds of Spring,
Already tasted in early Mornin',
By those who Observed their Masters seasons
With care 'n' reverence livin' in the green Wood.

For the Foreign had seen all this before
And were still curious,
In the knowing this was the first day.
Time, if time there is,
Had taken an' tamed this frequent visitor
To a World which is foreign, of Science 'n' logic
Far removed from His Lair.

Where a World of animal cunning still exists to excite
Haunting an' hunting like the Fox,
Hiding preying in our Subway.
An' there's a Cloud over the Sun.
Man what have you done?
While you wait to be freed
From life's rotating Spinning
Wheel.

# THE FLOWER

And does a Flower bloom 'n' grow
And speak of this in all its
Sweet 'n' scented perfume picked by hand,
Just to let thee know,
It likes the life amid the soil an' root
Where Man 'n' creatures all
Will come, though certainly
But to know a dream.

# THE REED

I am to be compared with a Reed,
An oh so strange Reed.
Standin' growin' in the grasses
Here amid the Marshes,
Stunted in all my growth.
Blown by the whining winds,
And drenched till I'm drown'd
Listening to hollow sounds
Of magic laughter coming from
The Jester.
Will the real face step forward
Please?

## DEATH OF A RIVER

As twilight came to these Sombre Western Skies
An' the mist sauntered in on the breeze,
During this ill fated evening tide.
And the stillness of the darkness did fall
About my person,
Pitchin' its black blanket upon the night.
                              As I stood alone,

And draped in my Cape,
Where the Words did Tumble
And fall,
Welling up,
As the Words of the River
Of life ran
Spelling binding,
And growing ever fearful,
Was the Poetry,

Because now Her death had Commenced,
Gaia The Ore,
Of that I was sure,
In full fast and flowing flood,
Crimson by colour,
Under many a-ancient bridge,
Through time and torrent,
Measureless to man.

For now Her Breath had been taken,
The breath that She breathed,

When Her Life giving Waters,
Those spirit of Waters so clear,
Were taken stifled 'n' strangled
By Plastic and Solution,
Till my Salmon, no more can Swim,
Home,
Home, from the raging Sea,

An' where is the Heron?
An' the Otter so few,
Together with the other Life
That was birthed from the Womb?

Oh 'tis dead,
The River,
Flooded with Life,
Flood with Oak,
English Oak,
Father,
Bering your own,
In trenches that are Foreign,
Where Sentences run, Teaming with Life,
For with Prayer They Begin,"Oh Crucified One".

## SPIRITS OF THE SEAS

Pebbles casts,
Seas sound like Ghosts,
Wandering the Earth,
With a murmuring,
Rippling.
To the Sea Shanty Tides,
         Turning,

Mending those Nets,
In spite your Thoughts,
In the Shells and Ears,
When two Worlds collide,
To a Gulls cry,
A Gulls cry,

Seas sound like Ghosts,
Venturing on to those old grey Rocks,
To Flounder and die,
With their Ships,
With their Ship,
Rolling out of the Mists,

And over our Bar,
The Bar,
Scrabbles you Wreckers,
To Take as you Will!
      You Will!

                                The N. Cornish Coast.

## THE ISLAND

It is the hauntings of Men
Who live in the shadow of its undoubtable wake.
For it is the last untamed brooding bastion
Even in high Summer,
Sometimes obscured in its own shroud
Of swirling mists, risen from the Seas.

The Island,
Stood strange 'n' tall with hypnotic charm
Hiding its face of Wildlife,
Where 'n' between brilliant Rhodedendron bushes bloom,
Cling, and hold fast to the rock
Sheer to depths below.

Few live upon the flat topped Moor like Plateau
Which is the Island,
With its Lights an' Church
And its shingle beach.
Though the great Norse Men came,
Used it an' named it.

Now Mr Jones 'n' other Twitchers they do come
Breakin' free 'from desk 'n' chain,
To use the Island as their escape.
Where once the Island 'twas used
To hide 'n' to hold Smugglers
And Convicts alike.
                              Lundy.

# HAPPINESS

Happiness,
>   Is just to wake
>   And find that the dark of the night has vanished,
>   And that the light of the day has arrived.

Happiness,
>   Is to drink the word
>   Like wine from the vine,
>   Pure 'n' sweet.

Happiness,
>   Is just a simple change
>   Of heart.

Happiness,
>   Is sweet soft rain
>   Upon my rose of Summer season passin'.

Happiness,
>   Is a smile, laughter 'n' a tear
>   All through the year,
>   Whilst standin' in the tunnel of time.

Happiness,
>   Is just to love
>   And to be loved.

Happiness,
>   Is just to have the right relation
>   With your Maker an' neighbour.

Happiness,
>   Is and Happiness was
>   When all is lost,
>   And all is found
>   Under the Tree of knowing bound in thorns.

Happiness,
> Is just a word made from seven letters
> Deducted from twenty six.

## THE ONLOOKER

A Park is placed strategically for Children's lark.
In the Park on grasses green
A figure tall 'n' lean.

Girl on a Swing wouldn't take
Any notice of the figure tall 'n' lean
Standin', if the figure had been a She.

He could see Her, rockin', swinging gently back, to and fro
Like the See Sawing wind an' the tide playing at
Political round abouts 'n' slides.

She gazed at His silhouette long an'hard
As He continued to remain
Firm, in the dew wet, soft wet of the grasses green,
His face covered, by falling shadows.

He watched as She stared back, harder again at Him
As She rode the Swing, Her Swing,
Her hair flowing dark.

Matching with the contrasting colours, of blue and black
Bright blue Sky, blue as the Heavens,
With a lurid pitch black, tarmac black, and "Ss-i-N" black.

She had been told of Men who stare

An' say nothing; calling for their desires into the wind,
For all that was now part of the game.

Now that She was round firm, and plump
Trapped in Her Tower,
His Tower, of mindlessness.

For He knew that She was the western Star
Arising, bright and brilliant, into Woman,
The Venus in His new Morning.

## A CONDEMNED MAN SPEAKS

All is worthless,
So why should I think of tomorrow?
By this time tomorrow
I shall be a dead Man,
And dead Men worry not.
Becoming one with the soil
Continuing to Spin.

So live each passing moment
Like the flower of Flanders,
Remembered, one with the soil,
For the grave is but an overcoat,
Shabby an' stained at that.

And from my Eye sees the view condemned
Of creatures mountains 'n' Sea,
Yet there is only one I destain
Man is He,
An' why?
For 'twas they who condemned me
An' this soil that spins.

## UNFULFILLED

Everyday in every way People 'n' places
An all their faces seem to look the same,
Gazing out in a melancholy way.
Taking on the colour 'n' form
Of drab 'n' depressive surroundings,
As they read their tarmac'd road.

I know all this, for I have seen them
From the top of the hill, together with the Sage,
Bearded an' white with age. He sits an' views them daily
Now that the Skies 'n' the Seas are no longer blue.

With His fading sight He senses that there
Is a cold chill in the air, and Men are aggrieved
Concerning those promises made in love,
And now lay broken like china from the cabinet.

Once upon a time He felt like them, did the Sage,
Whilst smoking the occasional good cigar
An' sharing the odd bottle or two
Along the way, though there was nothing He could do.

Whilst now He feels He has changed,
He feels He ought to speak
Now the crowd is gathered on their Park benches.
Yet He didn't listen, so why should they?
Knowing full well others have already dug their trenches.

So silent lips the Sage does keep, holding His peace,
Knowing the gulf is wide as young and old stand side by side.
They will learn as the pages turn, as He has learnt,
Now that His life is spent,
Nothing is really worth a cent.

I know all this, for I've seen them
From the top of the hill,
Now that we've come full circle.
Back to the time an' the place
Where decaying Autumn leaves
Wisp collect an' gather,
Around His old stone Tower.

## 2:53 A.M.

The building was strangely quiet
An air of hushed and well weighted expectancy
Had hung an' lay about for several hours,
Of this I could certainly tell.
As Her of the night was watched 'n' listened for
In the darkened ceilin' night World
That draped and came spiralling through.

For the building just heaved 'n' breathed
Moaning an' groaning living its life,
Quaking to the sound of those who lived within,
Now at peace, restin' an' dozing, dreamin'
In ignorance of slumber,
Carrying the Devil on their shoulders
Wrestlin' with pillows 'n' sheet.
For their day was still far off
And yet the noises of the voices could still be
Heard, Echoing 'n' bouncing around, jostlin' for
position,
Like words upon a page.

## DEAD FOLIAGE

Dead, dead and dead, are the leaves
As I whistle an' sneeze.
Colours all natures way
Greens and brown, yellows or gold.
Treasured memories of seasons past,
Collected to bag an' burn
Are these loathesome leaves.
Now just a nuisance
From twigs an' branches
Broken an' branded,
Raped clean by cruel 'n' cool
Sou-west winds, here in darker days,
Scattered upon Summer's lawn.
Now an Ocean mere, in a torrent
That pours.

## DEPARTING

There is no Engine, no platform
Where She waits,
No friend, no lover She takes.
Yes She travels alone,
For destination unknown
Through that night of Her departing.

# THE HANGING

They led Him out in chains and irons,
To the rope a-swinging from the Tree
They led Him out.
Like a Lamb He did go,
To the slaughter,
Like a Lamb He did go.
To the rope a-swinging from the Tree.
Where solitude is turned, inward Eyes
And those who come, they stand to watch
Jeering, in morbid fascination.
Amid the Clowns mumbled words
The straight Man throws His
Perfect weighted trap.

# THE WALL

When I finally hit the Wall
Then is the time, when time Will be no more.
And I shall see myself, and
Others for what they really
Are.

## THE FUNERAL

Our Morning was dreary an' terribly dismal
For those all wearin' black,
And black alone.
Even to the point of wearin' sombre Masks
To hide their laughs,
When the Bell it did toll 'n' toll 'n' tolled
Again.

For the Cortege drove slowly up the street
While I went and sat on My seat.
Others they talked 'n' talked aloud
Playing at silent whispers,
Never forgetting that they, dearly beloved,
Are mourning the passing of themselves.

# THE STONE

Is this all that there is of you
A stone standing, name
And the flickering memories of you,
To recall?
Though soon there will be nothing,
But the stone.
For those who remember will be as
Time, distant memories.

# RESTLESS SOUL

Now climb Down From Those Branches
Whilst Thou Still Can,
You Whose Heart Desireth To Know All Things.
For The Fruit Of The Tree Shall Fall Soon Enough.

# WAYWARD LIGHTS

A journey taken, now begun, on stoney ground,
Side the seeds and Ears of Golden,
Way, away from Morwenna and the Baptist,
Now one flesh you Pilgrims and strangers
That call,

See in their Garden of Stones,
Erect, Death white the Face of Caledonia
Is history past and in the making,
For the God of this age did blind the Eyes
Of the believer,
Unto the hills, from whence cometh their help.

With wayward lights, but for booty of violent passion,
All to grief on rocks of Cornish air.

Rev'd Stephen Hawker, 1834

# SEPTEMBER

September,
On the Wane,
Cools the Air,
Speaking of Summer still,
Reapers gather for harvest Moon,
Shadows Fall,
Amid the Rumour,
Tilts the Earth,
Away,
Away.

# THE BAPTISM

My first recollection of them was on the Beach
It was raining so I recall,
Anyway it didn't make much difference, wading
Through the waters of Baptism,
To be Baptised in to what? questioned the lone
Voice,
Father, Son, and Holy Ghost, replied the Wind.

Coming up they gasped, bound by Grace
Led by the Hand, their course was set,
Walking away no one knew.
And now they're gone, called then, to catch Men.

# SOMERS FALL

Autumn day, harvest, Autumn gold,
Taste,
Furnished burnished beech bronze,
Tinted in the shadow lands,
Mellow mists low where pleasant waters flow.

Reminiscences, toast of a Puritan past,
In hostelries now, built as stations then.
Colour my memory with your New Model Army.
A fragment lost like Somers Past.

Journey on to Dulverton, and the sound of
The distant rut,
Where the old clapper Bridge still stands to
serve and to span, the Barle, Trippers now.

Though at the Trigg spot, he light fades,
Way like my view, like my words running,
Like the river runs to the Sea, to the Sea.

## THE FLOWER SELLER

Once a Week they'd gather in the Market Square
Setting stalls sellin' their wares
Beneath those ticking talking hands
That just laughed aloud at Her weakness,
As She sat sellin' Her Flowers,
Sayin' "please buy my blumen".

Bent and broken lookin' on Her scars
Run deep in a distant face, and veiled tears.

Some said, She was a Witch being arthritic
And crippled in the hands,
Others said, a German, perhaps a Jew,
And they killed Christ, didn't they?
Eclipsing the Flower Seller and the love She
Would show with mute replies, And downward
Eyes,
Beneath those ticking talking hands.

Though She had seen the light, as they continually
Fed their faces making ready for the night,
Beneath those ticking talking hands.

## ODE TO THE FERRYMAN

Who Pays the Ferryman,
When the Ferry doesn't Run?

When the Tides all out,
And the Beach is all in,

When he's Drunk on Rum,
And Made his Crossing,
There on Jordan's Side,

For who Pays the Ferryman,
When the Ferry doesn't Run?

## AT HOME

Curtains are drawn, 'n' telly's on
Supper's done,
And Mr Smith 'n' Mr Jones are Home
To their own particular Kingdom come
To feud with Wife over bed 'n' blankets,
To wake come the morrow to bills and headline news.
Then the night is over the day has come
For Mr Smith 'n' Mr Jones meeting outside their
window
Where the walls are in ruins.
Only to be trapped leaving their Women at Home.

# REGRET

For several days I passed Him by,
That sad little old Man wearin' a frown.
Banging out His big bass drum, being the Clown,
And not a penny did I give Him,
My God, I wish I had.

# THE DRIFT

The frightened Foals rounded, penned, muddy
And now separated from Mother and Moor await a buyer,
Beneath the driving Autumn rain drowning out the Auctioneer.
First contact with Human hand, a stick hard across the back,
the price is fixed as the gavel comes down
And so the bargain is made complete,
And all know their fate.

# WALKING THROUGH THE WOODS

Beneath this turnin' canopy rain falls
Drip, drab, drip, as I pick my path,
Splish, splash, splash, through the unfamiliar woods
Changin' their faces with each turnin' season.

Gathered the Birds, Swallows to fly
Tree now fallen asleep, dead to the World and all Her elements.
Wind increasing, not quite the Winter.

Water flows, rapid, onward my destiny,
Keeps the narrow way.
With healing hands, knocked once in Father's Shop
Told Galilean Folk, raised, left His work to do.

## DUBLIN'S FACES

In from Wicklow across the sniffy Liffey,
With colour green,
Waves your winds of Orange,
To dance to fiddlers three,
And drink to the stone, where founding Fathers
Met to plot War against King George's Crown,
Whilst learned men studied hard in Cloisters
Of religion.

And all this time poor sweet Molly cries,
"Cockles and Mussels alive, alive oh, alive alive oh"

To Kitty's shame,

Way from Stevens Green,
Shaw, Joyce, Wild, and Yeats are all seen writing
Another verse,

Now kiss the Girl,
And say goodbye,
Goodbye,
By way of the Hapney Bridge,
Leaving their fare Costoms House once to arrive.

## DECEMBER STAR

Frost had bit the ground hard.
It stilled the night into a cold chill,
As I crunched my way across the crisp and
Well manicured lawns beneath the velvet skies
And December Star.

And as I journeyed on others came too,
Seeing the same December Star, burning,
But the heat from the flame did not diminish nor did its
Light as our night drew on.

Then the sound that we heard was that of Wood,
Hollow, and only Wood and nails knocking, to a
knocking tune
Sung to a Carpenter's whistlin' song,
So We then turned and went on.

## WHERE IS SHE?

Oh where is She?
Who ate with Me,

Oh where is She?
Who walked with Me,

And where is She?
Who Travelled with Me,

And where is She?
Who Began to See,

For Where is She?
Who held Me so!

Gone, gone like the rest of me.

# THE NOISE IN THE CITY

And everybody is doin' in the noise in the City,
To the sound of the internal combustion engine,
Honkin' horn 'n' pneumatic drills.

And everybody is doin' in the noise in the City,
When to chip the pavement artist a few bits
Looks a cool thing to do.

And everybody is doin' in the noise in the City,
To the beat of the Discothèque
Soup or a bed, and blankets for the few.

# I REMEMBER

I Remember,
>Boys in Tree House Dens,
>Girls in Navy Nicks,
>And Sunday afternoon Religion,
>Snotty Nose Kids,
>Now in Dead end Jobs,

I remember,
>Brass Bands,
>Loco's,
>Black and White Telly,
>Flower Power,
>And Reports from Nam,
>For then came the Man on the Moon.

## ELEGY TO COMBE

The Gulls are in land,
'Tis rough out to Sea.
There's nobody on the Pier except for
A few Fishermen, and they're always here
To a Man and to a season waiting for the big one,
Empty with echo.

And the Saints point direction in this life
Of storms,
Where a boat waits for the call for Men all at Sea
Acting out their rolls, against the Edwardian facade,
In these gardens that cling just below the tor.

## WHITE CAT

"Hi there"
Oh white Cat,
You're a Pub Cat,
Do you like Beer, Cider or Gin?

How many lives have you had?
Oh white Cat,
You're a Pub Cat,
Do you like Beer, Cider or Gin?

Why do you sit,
Silent eyes a-fixed?
Is it that you want some of my Plaice?
Or is it that I'm just another Stranger
                To your Face,

Oh white Cat,
You're a Pub Cat,
Do you like Beer, Cider or Gin?

                              The All Season Inn
                                      Bideford

## JANUARY FIELD

Birds seek as you might for that odd morsel or two
For the ground is hard and coated emulsion white.
Scaring winds cut sharp, burning swift
Like a mighty sabre rattling, rattling,
Through the naked trees.

Farmer,
Struggle through Shepherd of your Sheep,
They hunger layer deeper against the hedge.

And not far away lies something still
Food for others,
Having surrendered in front of the Sun.

## HERALDING IN

Soft Shoe shuffle 'n' ruffle
Over seasons memories spent.
Bark to bark where mosses cling
Down at edge beside the stream.

Fresh dew wet, fauna awake from Winter
Sleep,
Leaves whisper loud of Summer coming.
As light from light glinted and finds its
Way to Forest floor.

Nature busied Herself and song filled
The air.
Whilst in the town they danced and Crowned
Their Queen of May.

# RAILWAY JOURNEY

The Iron Horse, steaming Dragon has been replaced,
By Diesel click or is it clack spuring along the track.
Trundling on new horizons, backs of towns and no
Man's Land.

Dark tunnels black as night,
Dreams convey,
Seconds lasting,
Passing through,
Fellow travellers,
Perfect strangers.

## "SSHHH"

"SSHHH"
Empty beach.

"SSHHH"
Smooth pebble.

"SSHHH"
Calm, — Weed smells strong,
                "SSHHH"
"SSHHH" "SSHHH"
You can take my contraband,
                "SSHHH"

"SSHHH" "SSHHH"
I will wash you, wash you
                "SSHHH"

"SSHHH" "SSHHH"
And you are no more, no more.

# EARLY

To soar as an Eagle,
To wake upon the Mountain tops
For the crowds,
And view like a Kite, the Valley below
All clouds flow.
Black and silent shadows before the grey dawn,
Arise vapour mists,
Faced by burnished golden,
Wafting way like smoke,
Revealing pastures and Pines.

# NEWS

What is News?
Print on white, black on white,
That's News.

Pain and Sorrow, is but News,
Tagged with Sport, and Royal News.

She reads with stick lips, watch Her mouth.
Paid by the hour, People die by the Hour
That's News.

Like a child who writes its name on a frosted
Window pane,
and cries, HELP.

# UNDER A SAPPHIRE HEAVEN

Air still, not a breath blown,
Spoken though, under a Sapphire Heaven,
White building reflect on what might have been
Sounding out owners past and present,
Crosses carried, voices of the songstress
Tumbling in on narrow streets.
She sings and an old Man dreams,
She's fair and warm is Her heart,
Listen even the cobbles speak beneath the bells
Under a Sapphire Heaven.

## THE WAITING

We got married in a bit of a hurry,
Back last Summer Mum said I had to,
Need I say more, and now it's nearly autumn.
They said it would be over before Christmas,
We're not even sure which one now,
Nor can I be sure that He's still alive.

# STREAMS

Streams, streams of living water
Silver in their flow.
White over rock pour 'n' flow
Deep and coloured in their perception
Of us and us alone, reflecting, reflecting,
With and against the flow.

Faster the Stream, streams of constant tears
Way from source, you waters subside,
Knowing hearts bleed into time
For us and us alone, reflecting, reflecting,
With and against the flow.
White over rock pour 'n' flow
Constant to decree.

You stream to meet, rivers,
In Oceans you assemble, is love
Untold.

## EVERYBODY IS I

Empty Head, empty life,
Everybody is I.
Grab, Grab, Grab,
Spend, Spend, Spend
In a material life.

Empty Head, empty life,
Everybody is I.
Climb the ladder, need to succeed
Rainbows aren't illusions in a material life.

Empty Head, empty life,
Everybody is I.
Except the Dove, for all will end in strife,
In your material life.

## KATHLEEN MARY MCQUIRE

Beneath the Norman Tower,
Where the Shadow Falls,
Between the Twelve Yews standing,
Like Soldiers on Parade,
All Confederate grey,
Recording the age of Kathleen Mary McQuire,
Died – 1895 – at – 35.

Beneath the Norman Tower,
Between Twelve Trees Tall,
A Head Stone Stands,
Where Once you Danced,
Kathleen Mary McQuire,
Died – 1895 – at – 35.

Beneath the Norman Tower,
Where the Shadow casts,
Telling of Winters,
Endless chill,
Before you held that Babe,
'Twas your Own,
Who lived to Die on a Foreign Field,
For again Slate does not age you,
Kathleen Mary McQuire,
Died – 1895 – at – 35.

R.I.P
Weare Gifford
Near Bideford

## THE LONG HOT SUMMER

In the long hot summer below Hawksridge
Pools 'n' rivers evaporated, and grasses green wilted yellow tinder dry.
Under the unrelenting Sun, beating, burning, past experiences
Melted hand in hand,
During the long hot Summer, when Poetry spoke
Under the Willow.

## PRAYER

One prayer, two prayer,
Here a prayer, there a prayer.

One Man on a Mountain,
Sister sits silently,
And why?

When the Flame bums dim,

There is a need, to Speak.

(SUMMER OF '89)

# IN MY FATHER'S HOUSE

In my Father's House
He stands stripped naked,
So the World may see.

In my Father's House
There are tears spilt over dreams ashes of ruin.

Children looking for the morrow
And not for the moment.

## BEFORE

To stand in silence waiting for silence to speak as it does.

Before the busy away.
Crept music of the Birds,
                "PRELUDE"

# THE CHASE

The Pack surrounded the pink jacketed mount,
Eager for the Chase.
Gathered, the talk was of kills before and
The Chase to come.

In the copse stands the Stag, baying for
The Chase to begin.
Rivalling the horn, fearing the worst and
Warning the hinds,
Hearing the Pack in the wind.

There had always been the Chase,
Winners and losers zig zagging and doubling back
Through thicket, ford, and field.

Pandemonium was about to break loose to the
Outsiders unforgiving eyes.

## IT IS WHERE YOUR EYES ARE

Where is the fallen Sparrow?
It is where your eyes are.

Where is the changing of the Guard?
It is where your eyes are.

Where is racial discrimination?
It is where your eyes are.

Where is sexual immorality?
It is where your eyes are.

Where is love?
It is where your eyes are.

Where is the down and out?
It is where your eyes are.

Where is the street paved with gold?
It is where your eyes are.

Where is the Face of God?
It is where your eyes are.

## LOST INNOCENCES

Lost innocences,
      Is the realization that Santa Claus does not exist.

Lost innocences,
    Is knowing that the buck does not stop with Mum or Dad.

Lost innocences,
                                Sex.

Lost innocences,
                      Roses of Picardy.

Lost innocences,
                          Little Boy.

# TITCH

Did you see Titch on the Telly. last night?
He's got a Mum, He's got a Dad.
He admits to that, does Titch.
Livin' in the shadows, pickin' pockets, thievin'
Just like the Dodger,
A statistic — always — elusive, a — runaway.

(WRITTEN AFTER A 14 YEAR OLD BOY
HAD GIVEN AN INTERVIEW TO THE BBC)

## UNION STREET SUNDOWN

Darkness speed this night
As a twin tone masks the sad and soulful Sax.
Sleezy Saturday night 'n' fights,
Neon signs that beckon
               beckon

Hungry eyes,
She peels for them like a Banana tastes
               tastes

And the Blind Man He feels the tasty image.
Unlike the artists' eyes capture Her fat World.

Old Jack Tar raises another Jar
To His high heeled Queen,
Will He make his Ship come the Morning?
Will He make his Ship come the Morning?
Is a Gulls cry,
Is a Gulls cry.

                                     (PLYMOUTH)

# CHANGE

How the seasons change
Colours by decree, Wind fall,
And turn
All my yesterday, 'pon the circlin' Sands.

Water cleanse, setting free,
Spirit a - new,
Walls come tumbling down.

## THE LATE LATE SHOW

I sat propped in bed, watching the late late show
Around the midnight hour.
And the Singer sung Her Song, a testimony of youth
When the rain drops fell,
Had it been yesterday or tomorrow already.

# THE LEAVING

Parting shots through the S. L. R.
And long good byes through watery eyes.
Blown kisses 'n' gestures, through windows
As the engine purred and "RRREV'D" away,
Distance became the order………

## PEW MEDITATION

What would Christ think of this building?
Neat and Tidy - bells a pealing,
With Carving Ornate,
And Screen to separate,

Rest those Wings,
On your Word of Brass,
Stained this your Glass,
A Story told,
Your Prayer book unfold,

For God is an Englishman,
And quite a Tory at that!!

# JOY

You've done your Job,
Done it Well,
Feed Me,
Clothed Me,
Kissed Me Better,
And Patched those Knees,
Shared My Hopes,
And those Fears,
And now I've grown,
Found The Way,
Though Still yours – "Mum".

## THE BARGE ON THE BEACH

There it sits, its back broken on the Beach,
Weathered and rotting.
Its old proud Bow faces the point
And its ever present light,
Watching for the storm,
Now all play has ceased as the tide washes,
A well regulated clock,
Kept by its Master the Moon,
To the sound of bells across the Water.

(INSTOW)

## LATE NIGHT SHOPPING

Tonight is like Sodom and Gomorrah
People wantin' sleigh rides and snow.
The Kids want this, and the Kids want that.

He came for you,
And He came for you,
And for you.

(Voice of the crowd) "WHO?"

See Him lying on a bed of straw.

(Voice of the crowd) "OH".

                (ONE WEEK BEFORE CHRISTMAS)

## BOWEL MOVEMENT

Ever tumbling, descending,
Scores of Faces not one I know.

Ads are glimpsed, King size low tar,
In this man made Hell.

Sniff the air, charged electric,
Now rush of wind, Tin Tube appear,
Snaking through, from secretion darkness
Take Robots home to Suburban shore.

Heaven is there to be made in a necklace
Of cocktail parties.

> WRITTEN JUST BEFORE
> THE KINGS CROSS FIRE

## THE COFFEE SHOP

Cream Cakes,
And Waiting Girls,
Milk Shakes 'n' Soda Pop,
Bubble Panes, Brooches,
And Badges,
Sought reflected opinions,
From the Mouths of Embassy Intellectuals,
And so Our Folks groaned,
Whilst reading their Papers,
Watching the Automaton.
Coffee was spilt,
Looking out at The Asylum,
Chess was indeed being played.

The Lemon Tree
Holland St. Barnstaple

## LOVE IS?

Love is?
    Ridicule - nails in a Tree.

## DRAWING

What did the artist see when he drew?
Did he see the Boy who cast his net wide upon the water?
For his beard turned a ginger brown,
And has he reaped that which he has sown?
For friends are few and fools are many
Knowing truth through his weakness,
Loaned by God, Spirit blessed, Woman bore.

## SUMMER SHE LEADS US ON

A Dog leads his pot bellied owner.
A Boy drinks from a Coca-Cola can.

Whilst another dozes on.
Down at the Cricket leg before wicket,
Summer She leads us on.

A Child digs a pit, another builds a Castle
And looses the lolly that Dolly bought,
Summer She leads us on.

The artist admires the view,
Bronzed bikini clad beauties lie like beached
Driftwood, they'll be picked up,
Summer She leads us on.

To soft fruit 'n' the Centre court.
To Boaters and Blazers,
Summer She leads us on.

Tangled Weed and lovers lie,
As somebody cries, "that's the way to do it"
Summer She leads us on,
For She's not staying long.

## SISTER IN ARMS

The Wall is between you,
You Sister in Arms,
You gather and wait,
A Carbine cradle,
Clean is your babe,
Is this what you call liberation?
To die at the front,
Dressed as a Man.

# EQUINOX

And crunching Leaves,
Be Fell,
Misty Dew,
Fall,
Our Swallows have Gone,
Gone From the Wire,
To Love but another,

Though as for us alas,
We must face the Cold,
Oh Amber Friend,
Now in Shower of Rain,

With other breaths of
Likely Desire,
There is colour,
Draw Me ones Bow,
        Equinox,

Beside this Hearth,
Of ole Man Fire,
This Shorter Day,
Come Turning Year,
Of blissful Ignorance.

## THE FERRIS WHEEL

The Ferris Wheel goes round and round,
Turning, Rotating, Spinning,
Taking Trippers Higher,
And Higher,
And as for the Heights,
Well they make up for the Lows,
In a World of Indifference,
When the Bright Lights Shine,
Coloured is your Fair Ground.

# THE CROSS

The Cross it stands alone, against the World
For the World,
See your mascara run, oh Lady of the Street.
They have taken your Lord,
For the Truth it hurts doesn't it?
Like His Body broken with Sin.
Sounding board the rhetoric of the Word made flesh.
Angel voices sing, "He is not here, He is risen".

## JERUSALEM IN THE MORNING

Have you seen Jerusalem in the Morning?
Where the sun rises stirring the hearts of the Protagonist
Like dogs in the Deserts,

Have you seen Bethlehem's stall?
Where there's no Star 'n' Straw at all,

Have you seen the Jordan?
Heard the Voice and seen the Dove,
                    Descending.

Have you Climbed the Mountain,
And been in the Valley Trodden low.

Have you broke bread?
Only to see your Betrayer Come.

Have you felt the nails pierce?
A Carpenter's hands that healed.

Have you seen the Stone rolled away?
Knowing the Captives are free,

Have you met with your Master and Lord, Jesus?
The Christ,
Upon the Emmaus Road,
Then cast your Net wide,
Follow Him,
And Bring the Harvest in.

## SILENCE

Silence,

Not a Word,

Cut,

Like a Stone,

Skimming,

The Waters Cold,

And Plop,

Deep as Death,

Is your Silence.

# MEMORIES

Memories,

        Are meant to be greening,
        As the Summer,
        Like Manna of old,
        Spilt over,
        When Summer Shades that way,
        To Autumns Cool,
        For they are not meant to Waste,
        In Winter,

        Though to use Life experiences,
        Running over,
        Is your Spurting Fountain,
        Of Life most Lived,
        Is Colour,
        And Desire,

When you Loves Ones Memories!!

## MILL SIDE MUSE

I don't want to leave this place, I never do.
In this ever changing World, it always seems to stay
The same.

Listen now all I can hear is the Rooster crow,
And the Water flow,
But as for People, well they come and they go.

Ruled by those hands ever turning,
First to Sow and then to Reap,
Just as the wheel goes round 'n' round, round 'n' round.
Man's lot is an oh so dire one. He cannot escape the need
To have His fill.

Though Christ broke Bread once for all,
So Man may choose to eat and have His Fill.
Leaving His farrowed field, to gather in an even
Greater yield.

# SPENT OUT

Danny from Dumbarton had roamed a thousand miles of track,
And still not found direction,
Like the girl on the corner, left
Waiting, waiting with her rag tag bags in hand,
In the wasted years of this religious land,

They had heard the word, together with the angry young Man.
Shouting, shouting,
And still they're left to wander ,and why?
Shattered dreams fell like rain, upon the Orphans of night

Then Danny told his tale, again and again,
Crossing over the Girl wasn't in sight,
For the morrow had come, and bells began to ring!
When the angry young man, shouted, and shouted again!
"Jesus we need you"

## BREAKING CHAINS

It's how they sum you up,
A look, a gasp, with pity,
It is how they think you arc
And never what you arc,
For you're in the minority Lad,
And minorities can't fight back.

Whether black or white,
Rich or poor,
The stupid, the drunk in the glitter,
The one Parent Family,
Or just the cripple down the street,
Either way you're in the minority
And Minorities can't fight back.

Leaving you bitter, full of shame, like a dried up leaf,
Whilst the World it watches on,
And says, it understands.

Though there is one and only one,
who has climbed death's hill,
My brother my sister taking shame upon Himself,
Breaking Chains, His name is "Jesus".

Printed in Great Britain
by Amazon